Contemporary Rhythms

Volume Two
With audio examples available
on-line at www.muse-eek.com

by

Bruce Arnold

Muse Eek Publishing Company
New York, New York

Contemporary Rhythms

Volume Two
With audio examples available
on-line at www.muse-eek.com

by

Bruce Arnold

Muse Eek Publishing Company
New York, New York

Copyright © 1999 by Muse Eek Publishing Company. All rights reserved

ISBN 1-890944-85-8

No part of this publication may be reproduced, stored in a
retrieval system, or transmitted, in any form or by any means,
electronic, mechanical, photocopying, recording, or otherwise,
without the prior written permission of the publisher.

Printed in the United States

This publication can be purchased from your local bookstore or by contacting:
Muse Eek Publishing Company
P.O. Box 509
New York, NY 10276, USA
Phone: 212-473-7030
Fax: 212-473-4601
http://www.muse-eek.com
sales@muse-eek.com

Table Of Contents

Acknowledgements — v
About the Author — vi
Foreword — vii
How to use this book — viii
Example 1 — 1
Example 2 — 11
Example 3 — 21
Example 4 — 31
Example 5 — 41
Example 6 — 51
Example 7 — 61
Example 8 — 71
Example 9 — 81
Example 10 — 91
Example 11 — 101
Example 12 — 110

Acknowledgments

The author would like to thank Michal Shapiro for her patience and help in proof reading and for her suggestions. I would also like to thank my students who through their questions allowed me to see their needs so that I might address them as best I could.

About the Author

Guitarist Bruce Arnold has developed an extensive reputation as a composer and guitar virtuoso. His works are an original juxtaposition of 20th Century twelve-tone compositional methods and jazz improvisation techniques. In reviewing Mr. Arnold in The Los Angeles Times, Jazz critic Don Heckman wrote "Arnold's music never loses its contact with jazz and he deserves credit for his effort to expand the potential of the jazz palette." The New York Times has written that "Bruce Arnold could be the ultimate crossover musician." He has played with such diverse musicians as Stuart Hamm, Peter Erskine, Joe Pass, Joe Lovano, Randy Brecker, Stanley Clarke, the Boston Symphony Orchestra, and performs frequently with the Absolute Ensemble under the baton of Kristjan Järvi.

Both jazz and classical music critics have praised Mr. Arnold's most recent release "Duets" with French harmonica player Olivier Ker Ourio, a CD that combines musical styles to form its own identity; one that blurs the boundaries between classical, jazz, new age and blues. Newsweek Magazine reviewed the CD saying:"Imagine contemporary classical music, say, of Berg or Schnitke, played as if they were street blues."

Mr. Arnold creates his music with all the seriousness of any classical composer and close listening reveals it's riches. He has a unique ability to take extremely complex compositional theories distilling them down to simple beautiful music. Allaboutjazz.com has said in their review: "Duets" is meant to be admired from a close distance when time allows for a restful celebration of the arts."

Mr. Arnold is also deeply devoted to music education. He has taught at some of the most prestigious music schools in America, including the New England Conservatory of Music, Dartmouth College, Berklee College of Music, Princeton University, New York University, New School University, and City College of New York. Mr. Arnold is also the director of the New York University Summer Guitar Intensive, a program focusing on advanced improvisational skills and has created a complete educational line of books for this yearly event.

Mr. Arnold is the author of more than 50 music instruction texts devoted to crucial aspects of guitar technique, music theory, ear training, time, sight reading, and the overall mastery of high-level performance skills. He gives frequent clinics on many topics including: composition, improvisation, ear training and computer applications in live music performance.

Foreword

Many of my students have asked me how they can improve their comprehension and execution of rhythms. This book is an attempt to address their needs.

Although there are many books out that help you learn your rhythms this series of books is unique in that each exercise is accompanied by an audio example. These audio examples can be downloaded for free from the internet at http://www.muse-eek.com. The audio files use midifiles which can be played on a Mac or IBM computer by using a midifileplayer or any sequencer program. Midifile players are available for free at lots of sites on the internet, and muse-eek.com lists a few places where you can go to download this software.

This book is part of a sight reading series aimed at getting a student proficient at recognizing and playing rhythms. Other volumes in this series will introduce melodic shapes in different stylistic contexts. See the final pages of this book for a complete listing and description of current music related publications.

Bruce Arnold
New York, New York

How to use this book

The course of study presented in this book assumes that the reader has intermediate to advanced knowledge of music. With any course of study questions arise, therefore Muse-eek presents a forum where relevant questions will be answered by the author. Please visit the publisher's website at www.muse-eek.com first and check the FAQ section for this book to see if your question has already been answered. If not, use the form on the website to e-mail your questions.

Volume Two of Contemporary Rhythms looks at the notation methods of contemporary music. Composers in the last 100 years have departed from the traditional method of notating rhythms. This in turn has created a situation where you may find a rhythm you know but you don't recognize it because of the notation used. Obviously, it is important to learn to recognize these alternative notations to improve your sight reading ability

Although some of the notations presented for rhythms in this book are unusual it is important that you familiarize yourself with these alternate notation methods. Let's first take a quick look at how this modern notation differs from traditional..

The imaginary bar line is commonly used to divide music in 4/4 into two equal groups. If you look at example 1 you will see that it is difficult to see where the 3rd beat of the measure begins. In example 4 an imaginary bar line has been added making the beginning of the 3rd beat clear.

Imaginary Bar Line

Example 1 (Modern Notation)   Example 2 (Traditional Notation)

It is common in contemporary music to ignore the imaginary bar line. This is particularly true of common rhythms that a performer quickly recognizes. A common rhythm pattern is shown in example 3 which is then replaced by the modern notation shown in example 4

Example 3 shows traditional notation.   Example 4 shows modern notation.

 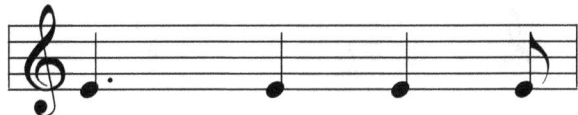

    Each exercise in this book progressively uses the imaginary barline less and less. It is common among some composers to ignore the imaginary barline altogether, particularly when a rhythm repeats over and over. Exercises 8 and 12 explore these departures from the imaginary barline to their fullest.

    Along with Muse-eek's series of books on rhythms I recommend reading a variety of different manuscripts. Over my many years of reading music I have found that manuscript and notation methods make a big difference on how the eye reacts when sight reading. In order to get your eye used to reading many types of manuscripts, go to your local library and check out any music you can find and read it. You will find that what I'm saying is true. Some manuscripts will be easy, while others will take time before your eye adjusts. Also try to find as much hand written music as possible. This will prepare you for those situations where you are working with people whose written notation is close to illegible.

EXERCISE 1

EXERCISE 2

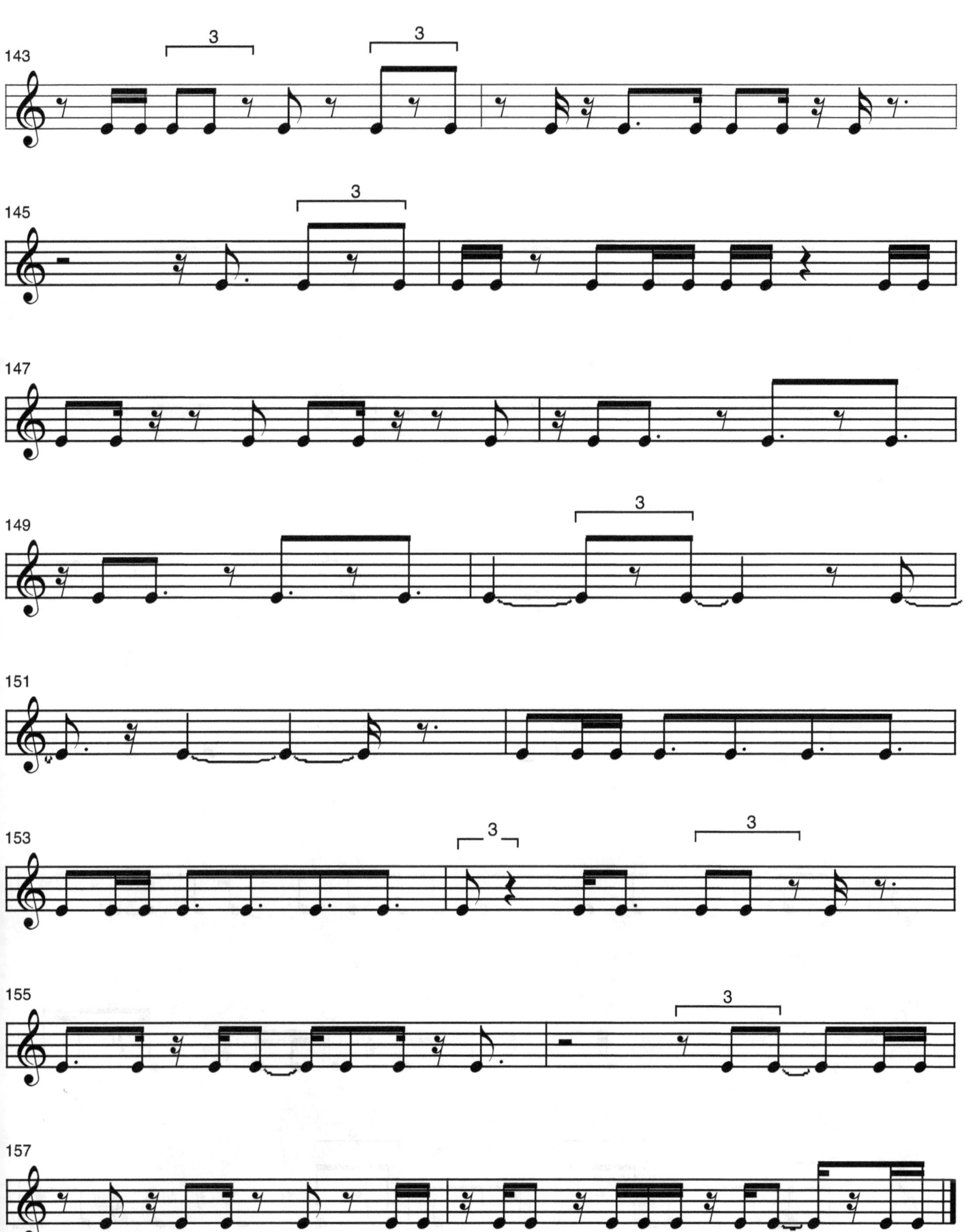

EXERCISE 3

EXERCISE 4

31

EXERCISE 5

EXAMPLE 6

EXERCISE 7

EXERCISE 8

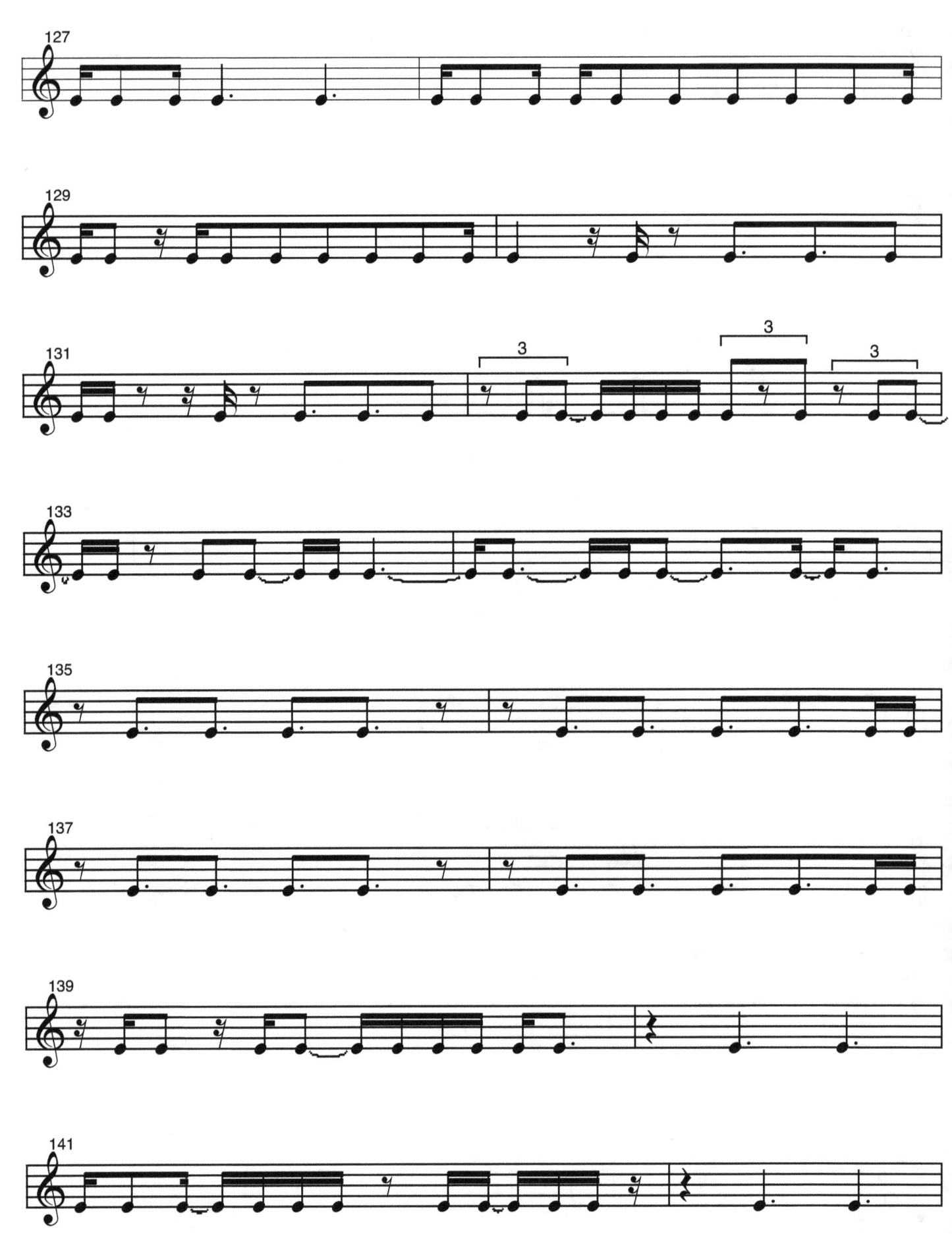

EXERCISE 9

83

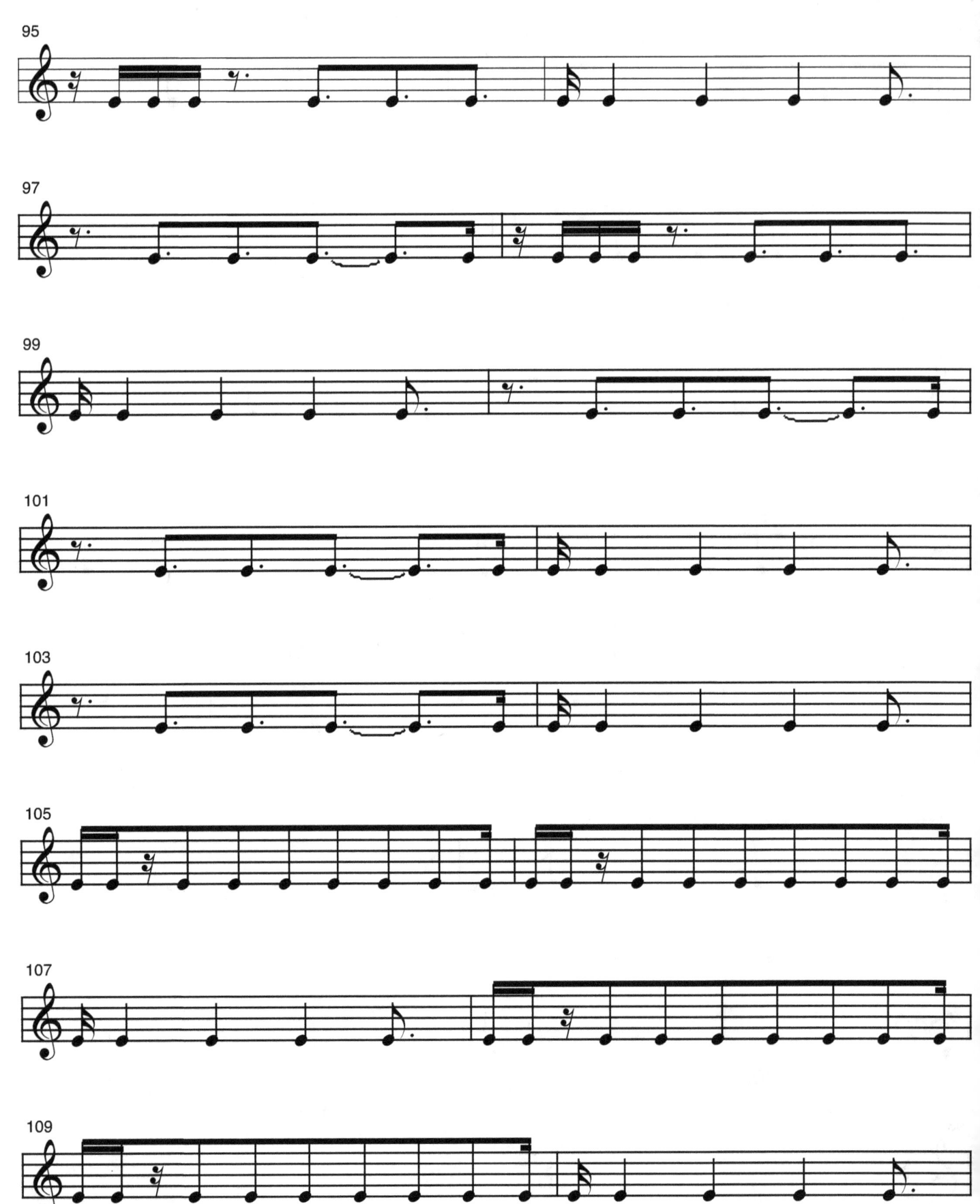

EXERCISE 10

EXERCISE 11

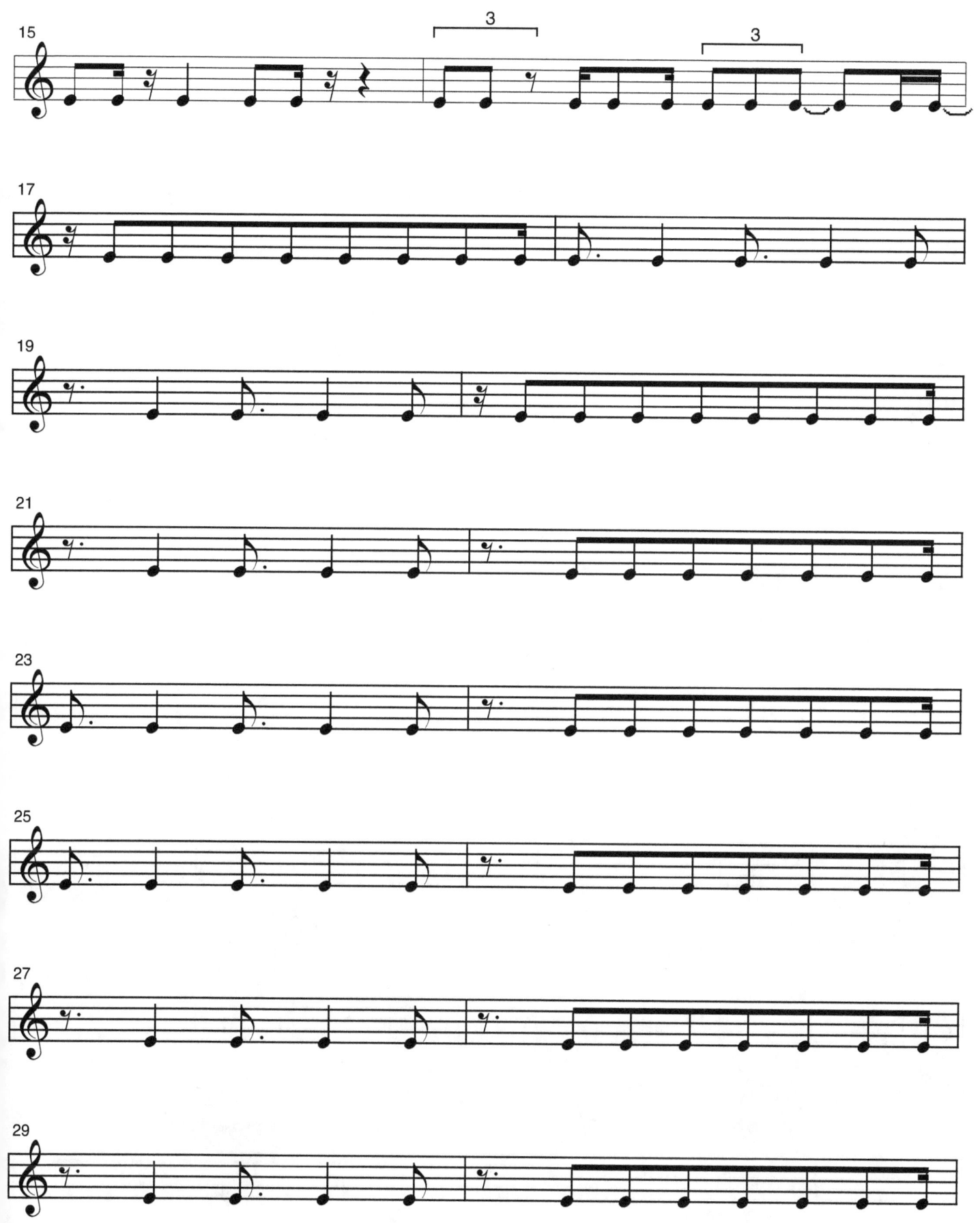

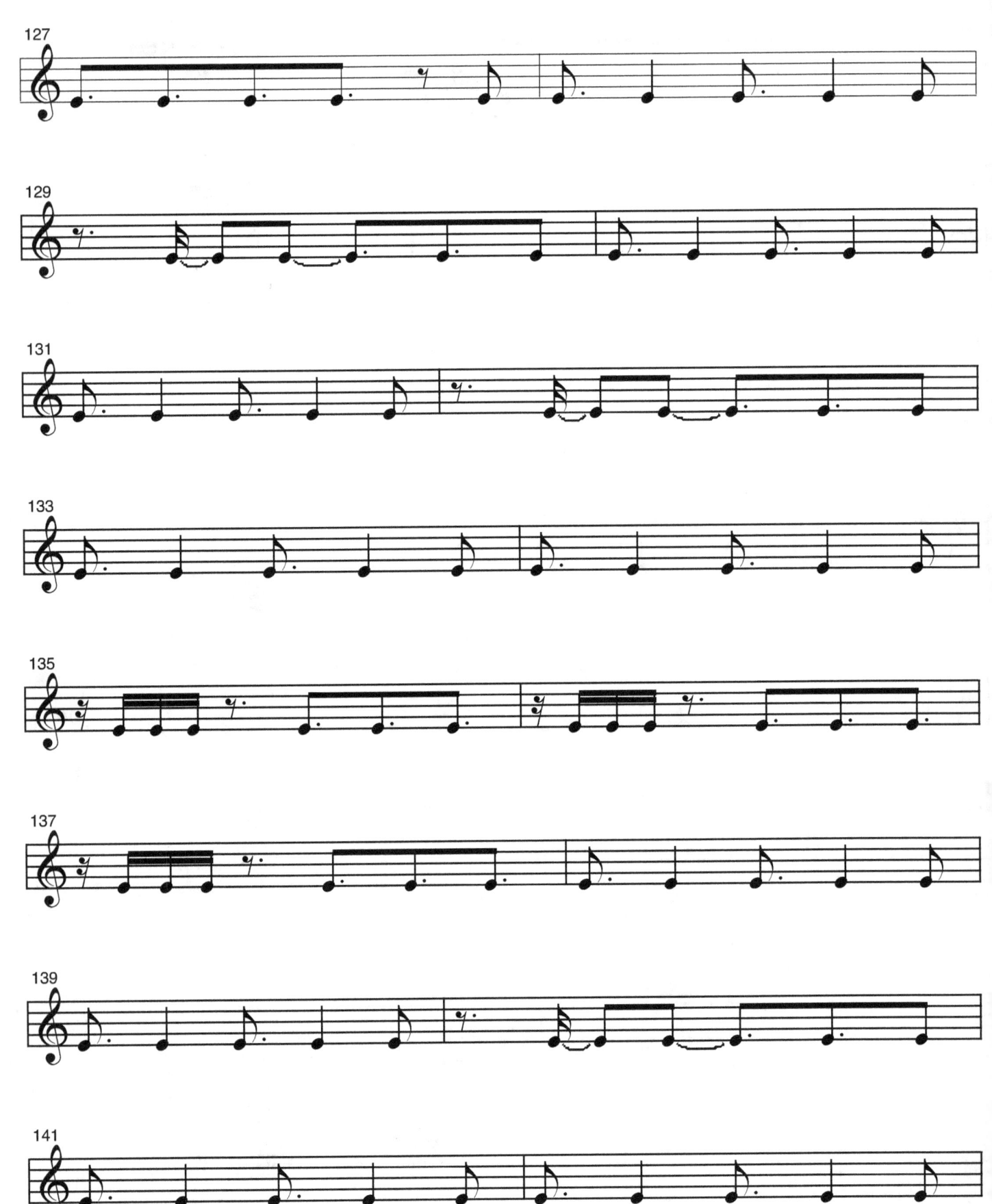

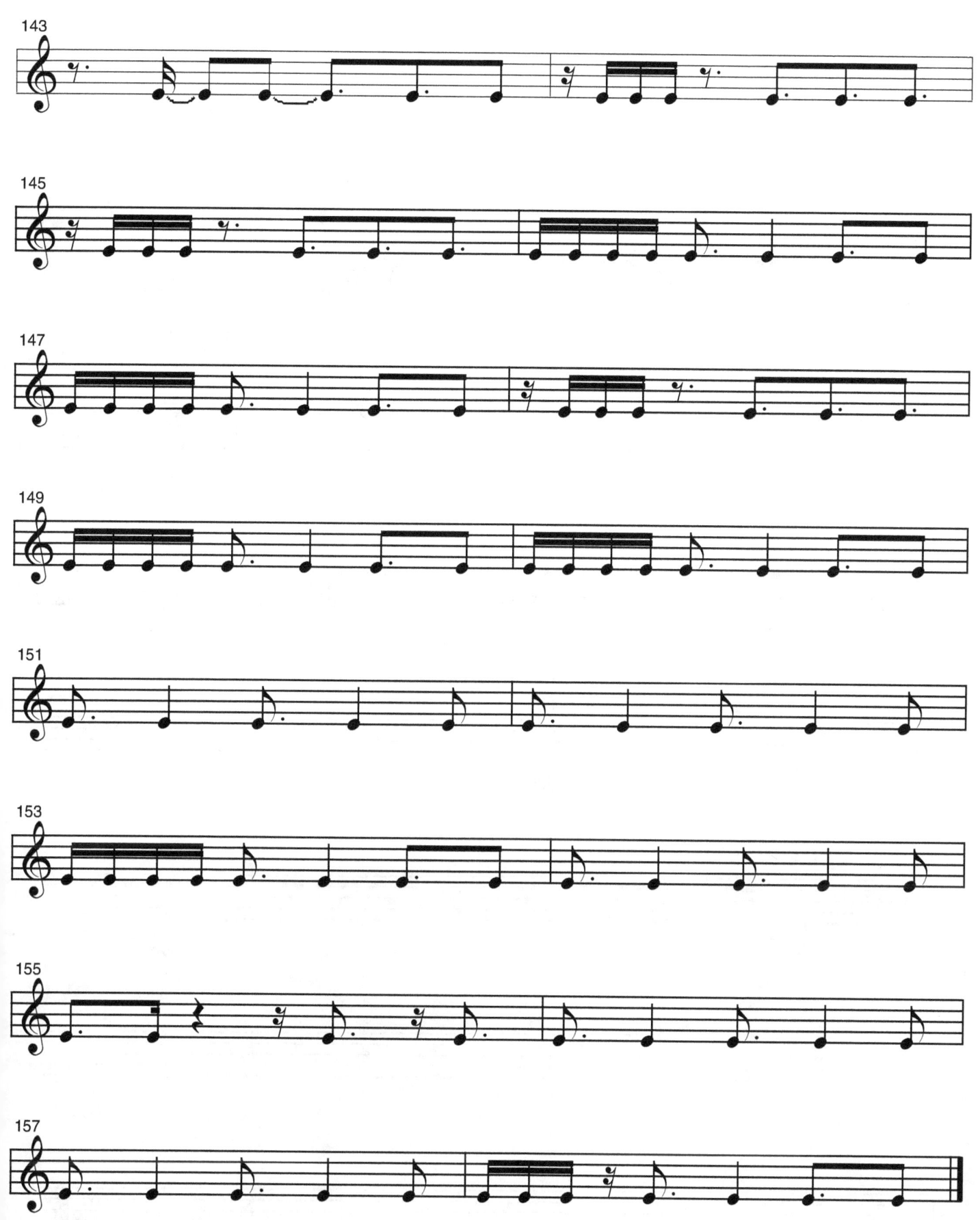

EXERCISE 12

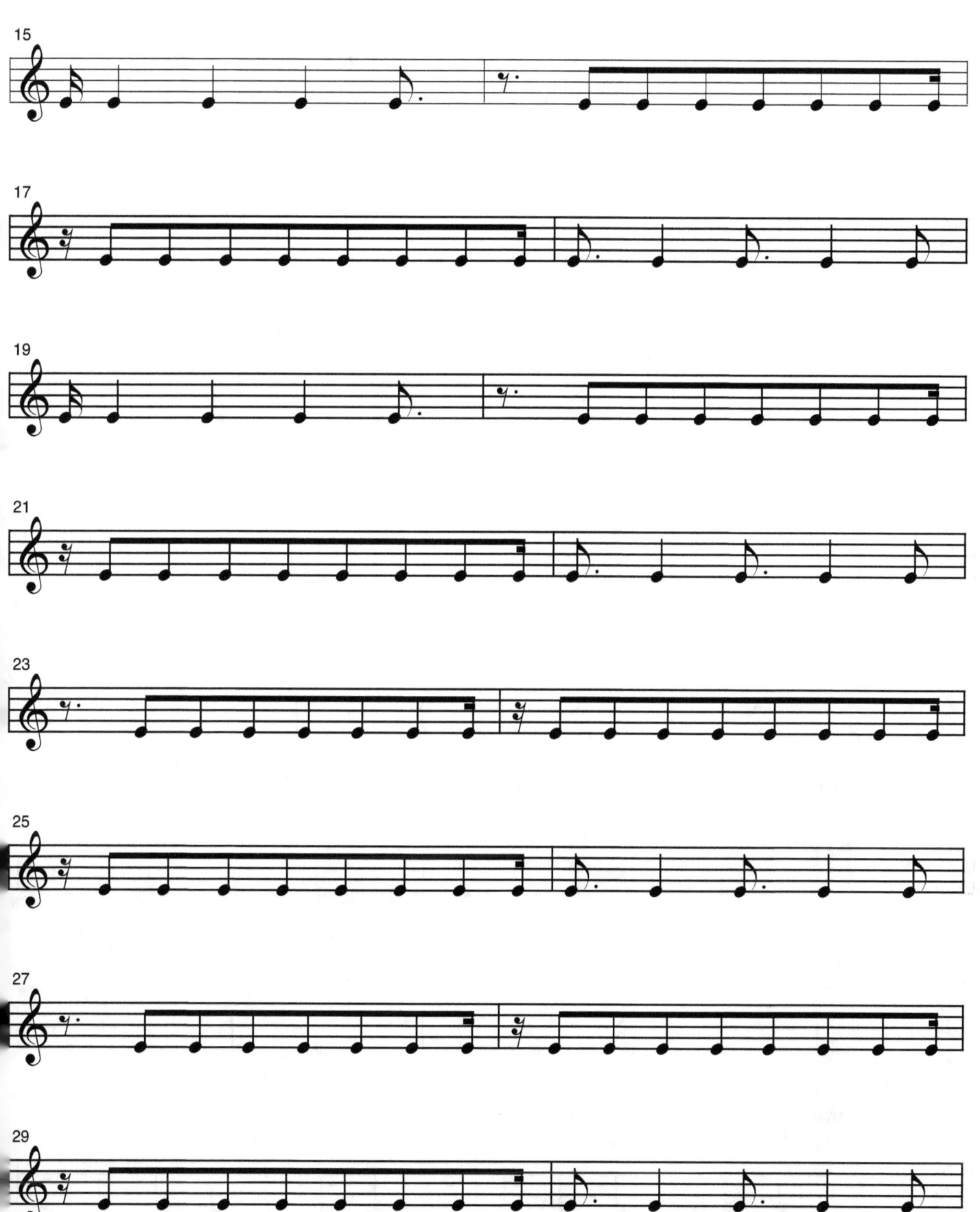

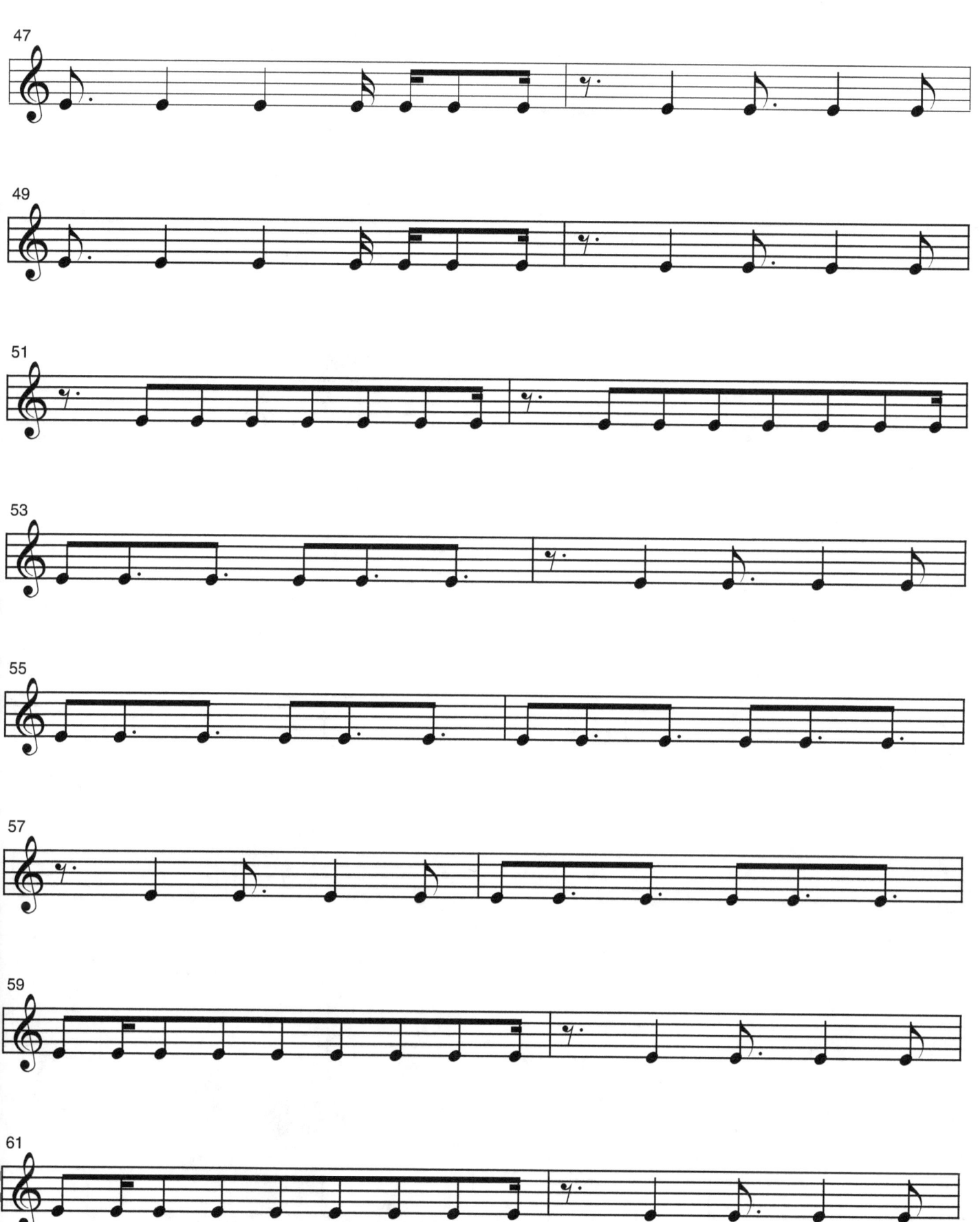

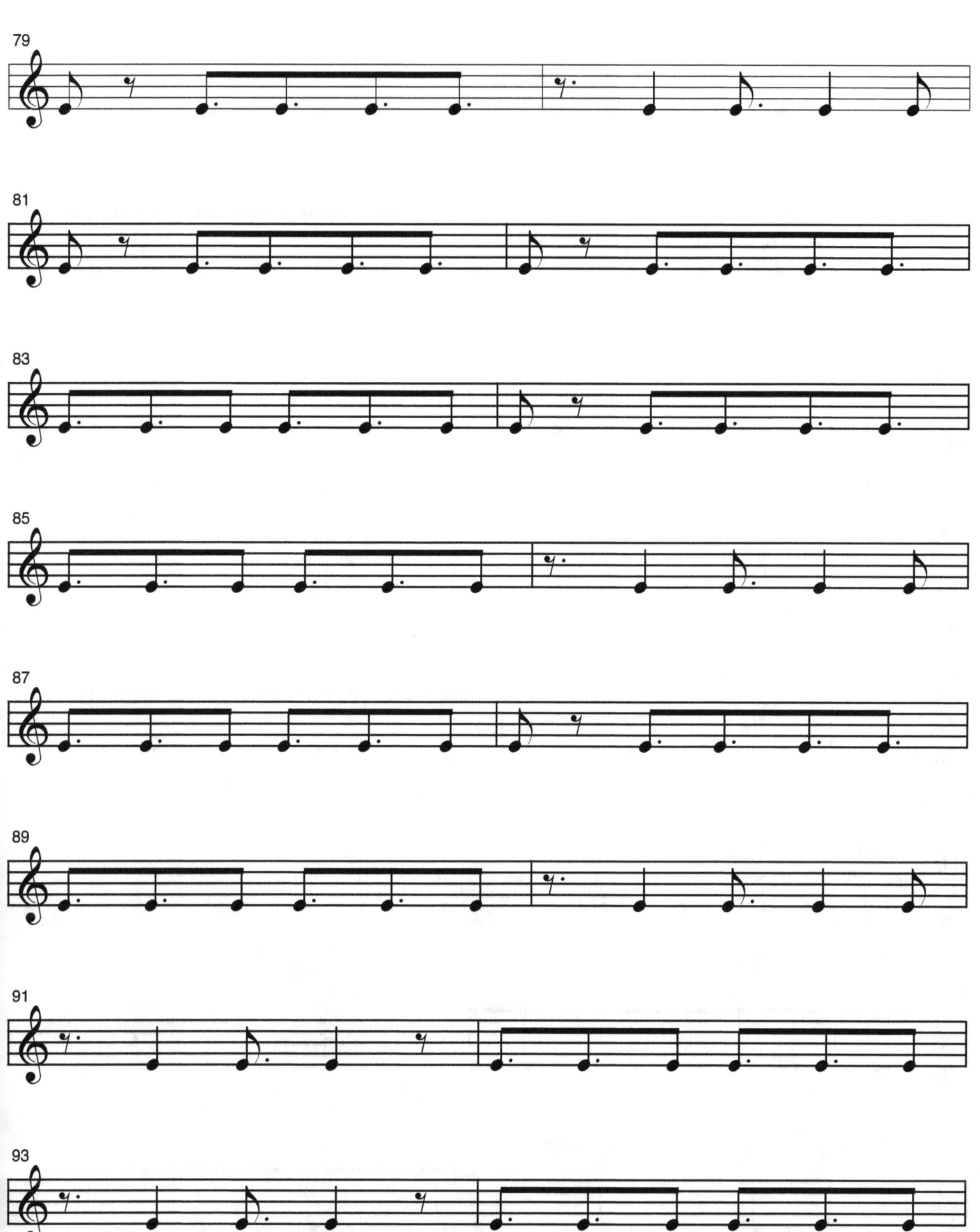

117

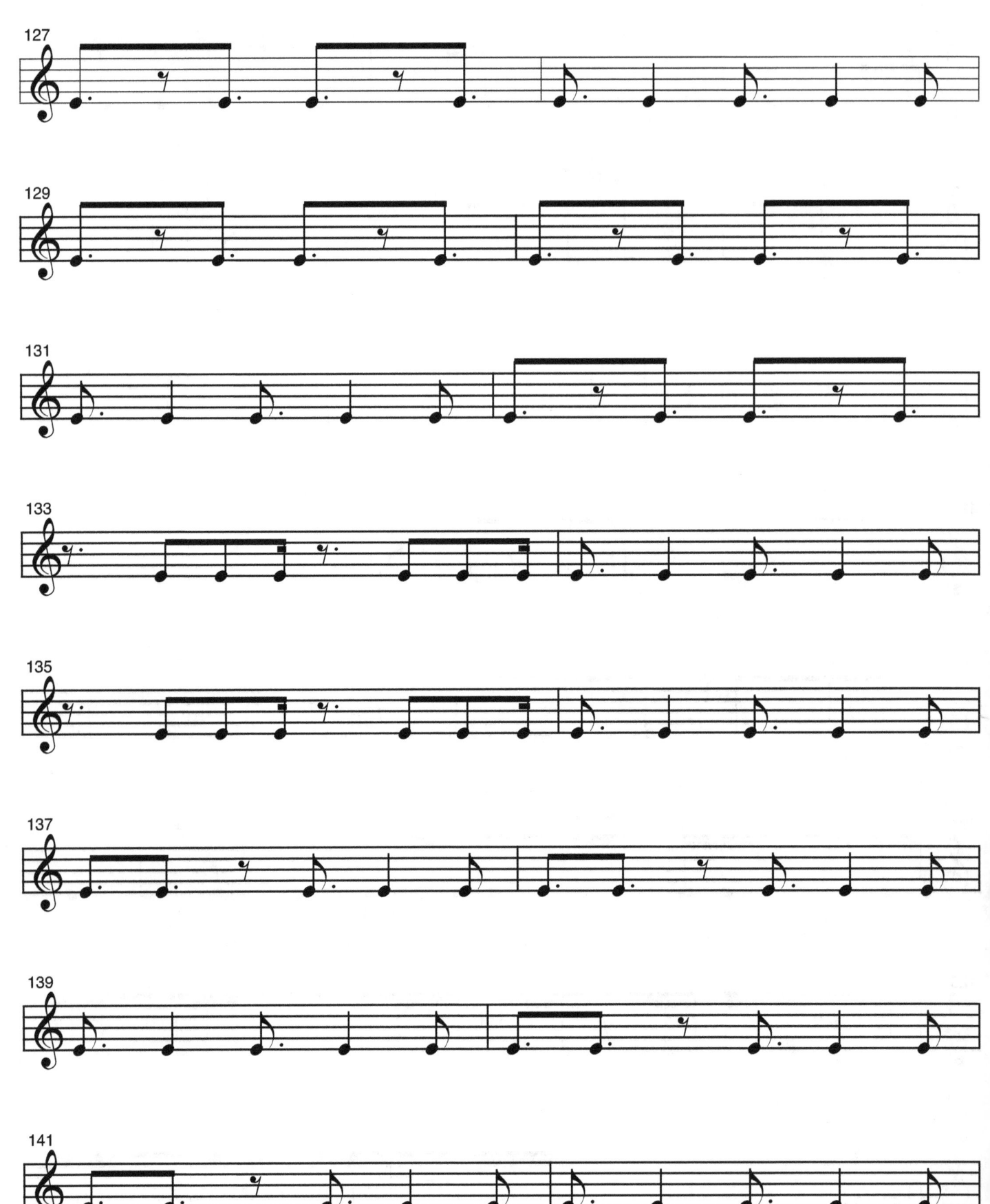

**Books Available From
Muse Eek Publishing Company**

The Bruce Arnold series of instruction books for guitar are the result of 30 years of teaching. Mr. Arnold, who teaches at New York University and Princeton University has listened to the questions and problems of his students, and written over fifty books addressing the needs of the beginning to advanced student. Written in a direct, friendly and practical manner, each book is structured in such a way as to enable a student to understand, retain and apply musical information. In short, these books teach.

1st Steps for a Beginning Guitarist
Spiral Bound ISBN 1890944-90-4   Perfect Bound ISBN 1890944-93-9

1st Steps for a Beginning Guitarist is a comprehensive method for guitar students who have no prior musical training. Whether you are playing acoustic, electric or twelve-string guitar, this book will give you the information you need, and trouble shoot the various pitfalls that can hinder the self-taught musician. Includes pictures, videos and audio in the form of midifiles and mp3's.

Chord Workbook for Guitar Volume 1 (2nd edition)
Spiral Bound ISBN 0-9648632-1-9   Perfect Bound ISBN 1890944-50-5

A consistent seller, this book addresses the needs of the beginning through intermediate student. The beginning student will learn chords on the guitar, and a section is also included to help learn the basics of music theory. Progressions are provided to help the student apply these chords to common sequences. The more advanced student will find the reharmonization section to be an invaluable resource of harmonic choices. Information is given through musical notation as well as tablature.

Chord Workbook for Guitar Volume 2 (2nd edition)
Spiral Bound ISBN 0-9648632-3-5   Perfect Bound ISBN 1890944-51-3

This book is the Rosetta Stone of pop/jazz chords, and is geared to the intermediate to advanced student. These are the chords that any serious student bent on a musical career must know. Unlike other books which simply give examples of isolated chords, this unique book provides a comprehensive series of progressions and chord combinations which are immediately applicable to both composition and performance.

Music Theory Workbook for Guitar Series

The worlds most popular instrument, the guitar, is not taught in our public schools. In addition, it is one of the hardest on which to learn the basics of music. As a result, it is frequently difficult for the serious guitarist to get a firm foundation in theory.

Theory Workbook for Guitar Volume 1
Spiral Bound ISBN 0-9648632-4-3   Perfect Bound ISBN 1890944-52-1

This book provides real hands-on application of intervals and chords. A theory section written in concise and easy to understand language prepares the student for all exercises. Worksheets are given that quiz a student about intervals and chord construction using staff notation and guitar tablature. Answers are supplied in the back of the book enabling a student to work without a teacher.

Theory Workbook for Guitar Volume 2
Spiral Bound ISBN 0-9648632-5-1   Perfect Bound ISBN 1890944-53-X

This book provides real hands-on application for 22 different scale types. A theory section written in concise and easy to understand language prepares the student for all exercises. Worksheets are given that quiz a student about scale construction using staff notation and guitar tablature. Answers are supplied in the back of the book enabling a student to work without a teacher. Audio files are also available on the muse-eek.com website to facilitate practice and improvisation with all the scales presented.

Rhythm Book Series

These books are a breakthrough in music instruction, using the internet as a teaching tool! Audio files of all the exercises are easily downloaded from the internet.

Rhythm Primer
Spiral Bound ISBN 0-890944-03-3   Perfect Bound ISBN 1890944-59-9

This 61 page book concentrates on all basic rhythms using four rhythmic levels. All examples use one pitch, allowing the student to focus completely on time and rhythm. All exercises can be downloaded from the internet to facilitate learning. See http://www.muse-eek.com for details

Rhythms Volume 1
Spiral Bound ISBN 0-9648632-7-8   Perfect Bound ISBN 1890944-55-6

This 120 page book concentrates on eighth note rhythms and is a thesaurus of rhythmic patterns. All examples use one pitch, allowing the student to focus completely on time and rhythm. All exercises can be downloaded from the internet to facilitate learning. See http://www.muse-eek.com for details.

Rhythms Volume 2
Spiral Bound ISBN 0-9648632-8-6   Perfect Bound ISBN 1890944-56-4

This volume concentrates on sixteenth note rhythms, and is a 108 page thesaurus of rhythmic patterns. All examples use one pitch, allowing the student to focus completely on time and rhythm. All exercises can be downloaded from the internet to facilitate learning. See http://www.muse-eek.com for details.

Rhythms Volume 3
Spiral Bound ISBN 0-890944-04-1   Perfect Bound ISBN 1890944-57-2

This volume concentrates on thirty second note rhythms, and is a 102 page thesaurus of rhythmic patterns. All examples use one pitch, allowing the student to focus completely on time and rhythm. All exercises can be downloaded from the internet to facilitate learning. See http://www.muse-eek.com for details.

Odd Meters Volume 1
Spiral Bound ISBN 0-9648632-9-4   Perfect Bound ISBN 1890944-58-0

This book applies both eighth and sixteenth note rhythms to odd meter combinations. All examples use one pitch, allowing the student to focus completely on time and rhythm. Exercises can be downloaded from the internet to facilitate learning. This 100 page book is an essential sight reading tool. See http://www.muse-eek.com for details.

Contemporary Rhythms Volume 1
Spiral Bound ISBN 1-890944-27-0   Perfect Bound ISBN 1890944-84-X

    This volume concentrates on eight note rhythms and is a thesaurus of rhythmic patterns. Each exercise uses one pitch which allows the student to focus completely on time and rhythm. Exercises use modern innovations common to twentieth century notation, thereby familiarizing the student with the most sophisticated systems likely to be encountered in the course of a musical career. All exercises can be downloaded from the internet to facilitate learning. See http://www.muse-eek.com for details.

Contemporary Rhythms Volume 2
Spiral Bound ISBN 1-890944-28-9   Perfect Bound ISBN 1890944-85-8

    This volume concentrates on sixteenth note rhythms and is a thesaurus of rhythmic patterns. Each exercise uses one pitch which allows the student to focus completely on time and rhythm. Exercise use modern innovations common to twentieth century notation, thereby familiarizing the student with the most sophisticated systems likely to be encountered in the course of a musical career. All exercises can be downloaded from the internet to facilitate learning. See http://www.muse-eek.com for details.

Independence Volume 1
Spiral Bound ISBN 1-890944-00-9   Perfect Bound ISBN 1890944-83-1

    This 51 page book is designed for pianists, stick and touchstyle guitarists, percussionists and anyone who wishes to develop the rhythmic independence of their hands. This volume concentrates on quarter, eighth and sixteenth note rhythms and is a thesaurus of rhythmic patterns. The exercises in this book gradually incorporate more and more complex rhythmic patterns making it an excellent tool for both the beginning and the advanced student.

Other Guitar Study Aids

Right Hand Technique for Guitar Volume 1
Spiral Bound ISBN 0-9648632-6-X   Perfect Bound ISBN 1890944-54-8

    Heres a breakthrough in music instruction, using the internet as a teaching tool! This book gives a concise method for developing right hand technique on the guitar, one of the most overlooked and under-addressed aspects of learning the instrument. The simplest, most basic movements are used to build fatigue-free technique. Exercises can be downloaded from the internet to facilitate learning. See http://www.muse-eek.com for details.

Single String Studies Volume One
Spiral Bound ISBN 1-890944-01-7   Perfect Bound ISBN 1890944-62-9

    This book is an excellent learning tool for both the beginner who has no experience reading music on the guitar, and the advanced student looking to improve their ledger line reading and general knowledge of each string of the guitar. Each exercise concentrates the students attention on one string at a time. This allows a familiarity to form between the written pitch and where it can be found on the guitar along with improving ones feel for jumping linearly across the fretboard. Exercises can be downloaded from the internet to facilitate learning. See http://www.muse-eek.com for details.

Single String Studies Volume Two
Spiral Bound ISBN 1-890944-05-X   Perfect Bound ISBN 1890944-64-5

This book is a continuation of Volume One, but using non-diatonic notes. Volume Two helps the intermediate and advanced student improve their ledger line reading and general knowledge of each string of the guitar. Each exercise concentrates the students attention on one string at a time. This allows a familiarity to form between the written pitch and where it can be found on the guitar along with improving ones feel for jumping linearly across the fretboard. Exercises can be downloaded from the internet to facilitate learning. See http://www.muse-eek.com for details.

Single String Studies Volume One (Bass Clef)
Spiral Bound ISBN 1-890944-02-5   Perfect Bound ISBN 1890944-63-7

This book is an excellent learning tool for both the beginner who has no experience reading music on the bass guitar, and the advanced student looking to improve their ledger line reading and general knowledge of each string of the bass. Each exercise concentrates a students attention of one string at a time. This allows a familiarity to form between the written pitch and where it can be found on the bass along with improving ones feel for jumping linearly across the fretboard. Exercises can be downloaded from the internet to facilitate learning. See http://www.muse-eek.com for details.

Single String Studies Volume Two (Bass Clef)
Spiral Bound ISBN 1-890944-06-8   Perfect Bound ISBN 1890944-65-3

This book is a continuation of Volume One, but using non-diatonic notes. Volume Two helps the intermediate and advanced student improve their ledger line reading and general knowledge of each string of the bass. Each exercise concentrates the students attention on one string at a time. This allows a familiarity to form between the written pitch and where it can be found on the bass along with improving ones feel for jumping linearly across the fretboard. Exercises can be downloaded from the internet to facilitate learning. See http://www.muse-eek.com for details.

Guitar Clinic
Spiral Bound ISBN 1-890944-45-9   Perfect Bound ISBN 1890944-86-6

Guitar Clinic contains techniques and exercises Mr. Arnold uses in the clinics and workshops he teaches around the U.S.. Much of the material in this book is culled from Mr. ArnoldÕs educational series, over thirty books in all. The student wishing to expand on his or her studies will find suggestions within the text as to which of Mr. Arnold's books will best serve their specific needs. Topics covered include: how to read music, sight reading, reading rhythms, music theory, chord and scale construction, modal sequencing, approach notes, reharmonization, bass and chord comping, and hexatonic scales.

The Essentials: Chord Charts, Scales, and Lead Patterns for the Guitar
Saddle Stitched (Stapled) ISBN 1-890944-94-7

This book is truly essential to the aspiring guitarist. It includes the most commonly played chords on the guitar in all keys, plus a bonus of the most commonly used scales and lead patterns. You can quickly learn all the chords, scales and lead patterns you need to know to play your favorite songs-and solo over them, too! The Essentials doesn't stop there, though. It also includes chord progressions to help you learn how to chord songs in folk, country, rock, blues and other popular styles. The books contain loads of easy to understand diagrams of chords, scales and lead patterns so you will be up and running in no time!

Sight Singing and Ear Training Series

The world is full of ear training and sight reading books, so why do we need more? This sight singing and ear training series uses a different method of teaching relative pitch sight singing and ear training. The success of this method has been remarkable. Along with a new method of ear training these books also use CDs and the internet as a teaching tool! Audio files of all the exercises are easily downloaded from the internet at www.muse-eek.com By combining interactive audio files with a new approach to ear training a student's progress is limited only by their willingness to practice!

A Fanatic's Guide to Ear Training and Sight Singing
Spiral Bound ISBN 1-890944-19-X   Perfect Bound ISBN 1890944-75-0

This book and CD present a method for developing good pitch recognition through sight singing. This method differs from the myriad of other sight singing books in that it develops the ability to identify and name all twelve pitches within a key center. Through this method a student gains the ability to identify sound based on it's relationship to a key and not the relationship of one note to another (i.e. interval training as commonly taught in many texts). All note groupings from one to six notes are presented giving the student a thesaurus of basic note combinations which develops sight singing and note recognition to a level unattainable before this Guide's existence.

Key Note Recognition
Spiral Bound ISBN 1-890944-30-3   Perfect Bound ISBN 1890944-77-7

This book and CD present a method for developing the ability to recognize the function of any note against a key. This method is a must for anyone who wishes to sound one note on an instrument or voice and instantly know what key a song is in. Through this method a student gains the ability to identify a sound based on its relationship to a key and not the relationship of one note to another (i.e. interval training as commonly taught in many texts). Key Center Recognition is a definite requirement before proceeding to two note ear training.

LINES Volume One: Sight Reading and Sight Singing Exercises
Spiral Bound ISBN 1-890944-09-2   Perfect Bound ISBN 1890944-76-9

This book can be used for many applications. It is an excellent source for easy half note melodies that a beginner can use to learn how to read music or for sight singing slightly chromatic lines. An intermediate or advanced student will find exercises for multi-voice reading. These exercises can also be used for multi-voice ear training. The book has the added benefit in that all exercises can be heard by downloading the audio files for each example. See http://www.muse-eek.com for details.

LINES Volume Two: Sight Reading and Sight Singing Exercises
Spiral Bound ISBN 1-594899-88-6   Perfect Bound ISBN 1594899-99-1

Recommended for those who have completed volume one, volume two introduces more complex harmonic material. This book can be used for many applications. It is an excellent source for easy quarter note melodies that a beginner can use to learn how to read music or for sight singing slightly chromatic lines. An intermediate or advanced student will find exercises for multi-voice reading. These exercises can also be used for multi-voice ear training. The book has the added benefit in that all exercises can be heard by downloading the audio files for each example. See http://www.muse-eek.com for details.

Ear Training ONE NOTE: Beginning Level
Spiral Bound ISBN 1-890944-12-2   Perfect Bound ISBN 1890944-66-1

This Book and Audio CD presents a new and exciting method for developing relative pitch ear training. It has been used with great success and is now finally available on CD. There are three levels available depending on the student's ability. This beginning level is recommended for students who have little or no music training.

Ear Training ONE NOTE: Intermediate Level
Spiral Bound ISBN 1-890944-13-0   Perfect Bound ISBN 1890944-67-X

      This Audio CD and booklet presents a new and exciting method of developing relative pitch ear training. It has been used with great success and is now finally available on CD. This intermediate level is recommended for students who have had some music training but still find their skills need more development.

Ear Training ONE NOTE: Advanced Level
Spiral Bound ISBN 1-890944-14-9   Perfect Bound ISBN 1890944-68-8

      This Audio CD and booklet presents a new and exciting method of developing relative pitch ear training. It has been used with great success and is now finally available on CD. There are three levels available depending on the student's ability. This advanced level is recommended for students who have worked with the intermediate level and now wish to perfect their skills.

Ear Training TWO NOTE: Beginning Level Volume One
Spiral Bound ISBN 1-890944-31-9   Perfect Bound ISBN 1890944-69-6

      This Book and Audio CD continues the method of developing relative pitch ear training as set forth in the "Ear Training, One Note" series. There are six volumes in the beginning level series. Through practice, the student eventually gains the ability to recognize the key and the names of any two notes played simultaneously. Volume One concentrates on 5ths. Prerequisite: a strong grasp of the One Note method.

Ear Training TWO NOTE: Beginning Level Volume Two
Spiral Bound ISBN 1-890944-32-7   Perfect Bound ISBN 1890944-70-X

      This Book and Audio CD continues the method of developing relative pitch ear training as set forth in the "Ear Training, One Note" series. There are six volumes in the beginning level series. Through practice, the student eventually gains the ability to recognize the key and the names of any two notes played simultaneously. Volume Two concentrates on 3rds. Prerequisite: a strong grasp of the One Note method.

Ear Training TWO NOTE: Beginning Level Volume Three
Spiral Bound ISBN 1-890944-33-5   Perfect Bound ISBN 1890944-71-8

      This Book and Audio CD continues the method of developing relative pitch ear training as set forth in the "Ear Training, One Note" series. There are six volumes in the beginning level series. Through practice, the student eventually gains the ability to recognize the key and the names of any two notes played simultaneously. Volume Three concentrates on 6ths. Prerequisite: a strong grasp of the One Note method.

Ear Training TWO NOTE: Beginning Level Volume Four
Spiral Bound ISBN 1-890944-34-3   Perfect Bound ISBN 1890944-72-6

      This Book and Audio CD continues the method of developing relative pitch ear training as set forth in the "Ear Training, One Note" series. There are six volumes in the beginning level series. Through practice, the student eventually gains the ability to recognize the key and the names of any two notes played simultaneously. Volume Four concentrates on 4ths. Prerequisite: a strong grasp of the One Note method.

Ear Training TWO NOTE: Beginning Level Volume Five
Spiral Bound ISBN 1-890944-35-1   Perfect Bound ISBN 1890944-73-4

This Book and Audio CD continues the method of developing relative pitch ear training as set forth in the "Ear Training, One Note" series. There are six volumes in the beginning level series. Through practice, the student eventually gains the ability to recognize the key and the names of any two notes played simultaneously. Volume Five concentrates on 2nds. Prerequisite: a strong grasp of the One Note method.

Ear Training TWO NOTE: Beginning Level Volume Six
Spiral Bound ISBN 1-890944-36-X   Perfect Bound ISBN 1890944-74-2

This Book and Audio CD continues the method of developing relative pitch ear training as set forth in the "Ear Training, One Note" series. There are six volumes in the beginning level series. Through practice, the student eventually gains the ability to recognize the key and the names of any two notes played simultaneously. Volume Six concentrates on 7ths. Prerequisite: a strong grasp of the One Note method.

Comping Styles Series

This series is built on the progressions found in Chord Workbook Volume One. Each book covers a specific style of music and presents exercises to help a guitarist, bassist or drummer master that style. Audio CDs are also available so a student can play along with each example and really get "into the groove."

Comping Styles for the Guitar Volume Two FUNK
Spiral Bound ISBN 1-890944-07-6   Perfect Bound ISBN 1890944-60-2

This volume teaches a student how to play guitar or piano in a funk style. 36 Progressions are presented: 12 keys of a Major and Minor Blues plus 12 keys of Rhythm Changes A different groove is presented for each exercise giving the student a wide range of funk rhythms to master. An Audio CD is also included so a student can play along with each example and really get "into the groove." The audio CD contains "trio" versions of each exercise with Guitar, Bass and Drums.

Comping Styles for the Bass Volume Two FUNK
Spiral Bound ISBN 1-890944-08-4   Perfect Bound ISBN 1890944-61-0

This volume teaches a student how to play bass in a funk style. 36 Progressions are presented: 12 keys of a Major and Minor Blues plus 12 keys of Rhythm Changes A different groove is presented for each exercise giving the student a wide range of funk rhythms to master. An Audio CD is also included so a student can play along with each example and really get "into the groove." The audio CD contains "trio" versions of each exercise with Guitar, Bass and Drums.

Jazz and Blues Bass Line
Spiral Bound ISBN 1-890944-15-7   Perfect Bound ISBN 1890944-16-5

This book covers the basics of bass line construction. A theoretical guide to building bass lines is presented along with 36 chord progressions utilizing the twelve keys of a Major and Minor Blues, plus twelve keys of Rhythm Changes. A reharmonization section is also provided which demonstrates how to reharmonize a chord progression on the spot.

Time Series

The Doing Time series presents a method for contacting, developing and relying on your internal time sense: This series is an excellent resource for any musician who is serious about developing strong internal sense of time. This is particularly useful in any kind of music where the rhythms and time signatures may be very complex or free, and there is no conductor.

THE BIG METRONOME
Spiral Bound ISBN 1-890944-37-8   Perfect Bound ISBN 1890944-82-3

The Big Metronome is designed to help you develop a better internal sense of time. This is accomplished by requiring you to "feel time" rather than having you rely on the steady click of a metronome. The idea is to slowly wean yourself away from an external device and rely on your internal/natural sense of time. The exercises presented work in conjunction with the three CDs that accompany this book. CD 1 presents the first 13 settings from a traditional metronome 40-66; the second CD contains metronome markings 69-116, and the third CD contains metronome markings 120-208. The first CD gives you a 2 bar count off and a click every measure, the second CD gives you a 2 bar count off and a click every 2 measures, the 3rd CD gives you a 2 bar count off and a click every 4 measures. By presenting all common metronome markings a student can use these 3 CDs as a replacement for a traditional metronome.

Doing Time with the Blues Volume One
Spiral Bound ISBN 1-890944-17-3   Perfect Bound ISBN 1890944-78-5

The book and CD presents a method for gaining an internal sense of time thereby eliminating dependence on a metronome. The book presents the basic concept for developing good time and also includes exercises that can be practiced with the CD. The CD provides eight 8 minute tracks at different tempos in which the time is delineated every 2 bars, and with an extra hit every 12 bars to outline the blues form. The student may then use the exercises presented in the book to gain control of their execution or improvise to gain control of their ideas using this bare minimum of time delineation.

Doing Time with the Blues Volume Two
Spiral Bound ISBN 1-890944-18-1   Perfect Bound ISBN 1890944-79-3

This is the 2nd volume of a four volume series which presents a method for developing a musicians internal sense of time, thereby eliminating dependence on a metronome. This 2nd volume presents different exercises which further the development of this time sense. This 2nd volume begins to test even a professional level players ability. The CD provides eight 8 minute tracks at different tempos in which the time is delineated every 4 bars with an extra hit every 12 bars to outline the blues form. New exercises are also included that can be practiced with the CD. This series is an excellent resource for any musician who is serious about developing an internal sense of time.

Doing Time with 32 Bars Volume One
Spiral Bound ISBN 1-890944-22-X   Spiral Bound ISBN 1890944-80-7

      The book and CD presents a method for gaining an internal sense of time thereby eliminating dependence on a metronome. The book presents the basic concept for developing good time and also includes exercises that can be practiced with the CD. The CD provides eight 8 minute tracks at different tempos in which the time is delineated every 2 bars, with an extra hit every 32 to outline the 32 bar form. The student may then use the exercises presented in the book to gain control of their execution or improvise to gain control of their ideas using this bare minimum of time delineation.

Doing Time with 32 Bars Volume Two
Spiral Bound ISBN 1-890944-23-8   Spiral Bound ISBN 1890944-81-5

      This is the 2nd volume of a four volume series which presents a method for developing a musicians internal sense of time, thereby eliminating dependence on a metronome.. This 2nd volume presents different exercises which further the development of this time sense. This 2nd volume begins to test even a professional level players ability. The CD provides eight 8 minute tracks at different tempos in which the time is delineated every 4 bars with an extra hit every 32 bars to outline the 32 bar form.   New exercises are also included that can be practiced with the CD. This series is an excellent resource for any musician who is serious about developing an internal sense of time.

Time Transformation
Spiral Bound ISBN 1594899-929-0   Perfect Bound ISBN 1594899-930-4

      "Time Transformation" is designed to take the application of odd meters to another level of mastery. Etudes are presented in 12 keys using the time signatures of 3/4, 4/4, 5/4, 6/4 and 7/4. There are a total of 60 highly syncopated studies that are presented using various combinations of eighth note and sixteenth note rhythms. Book also includes downloadable "vamps" that can be used in various ways with each étude.

Other Workbooks

Music Theory Workbook for All Instruments, Volume 1: Interval and Chord Construction
Spiral Bound ISBN 1594899-51-7   Perfect Bound ISBN 1890944-46-7

      This book provides real hands-on application of intervals and chords. A theory section written in concise and easy to understand language prepares the student for all exercises. Worksheets are given that quiz a student about intervals and chord construction using staff notation. Answers are supplied in the back of the book enabling a student to work without a teacher.

Jazz Piano Vocabulary by Roberta Piket, Volume 1: The Major Scale
Spiral Bound ISBN 1594899-51-7   Perfect Bound ISBN 1594899-51-7

      This is the 1st volume in a series designed to help the student of jazz piano learn and apply jazz scales by mastering each scale and its uses in improvisation. Each book focuses on a different scale, illustrating the scale in all twelve keys with complete fingerings. Also provided are chords and left hand voicings to match, exercises and études to apply the material to improvising, ideas for further study and listening, and detailed suggestions on how to prace the material. Volume 1 also includes a detailed primer in note reading, basic theory, and rhythmic notation.

Jazz Piano Vocabulary by Roberta Piket, Volume 2: The Dorian Mode
Spiral Bound ISBN 1890944-96-3   Perfect Bound ISBN 1890944-98-X

The 2nd volume in the series, this book focuses on the Dorian scale and applies it to improvising on minor seventh chords. The Dorian scale is presented in all twelve keys with complete fingerings. The book also contains left hand voicings, exercises, many examples, an étude to help apply the material, ideas for further study, an extended discography, and detailed instruction and practice tips.

Jazz Piano Vocabulary by Roberta Piket, Volume 3: The Phrygian Mode
Spiral Bound ISBN 1594899-53-3   Perfect Bound ISBN 1594899-54-1

For students who have covered the basics in Volume 1,2 and 5, this book focuses in the Phrygian and Spanish Phrygian scales. It discusses "modern" jazz chords such as the "Phrygian" chord (susb9). The scale is presented in all 12 keys with fingerings. It also provides a detailed treatise on a modal approach to chord voicings, practice tips and a Phrygian étude.

Jazz Piano Vocabulary by Roberta Piket, Volume 4: The Lydian Mode
Spiral Bound ISBN 1594899-55-X   Perfect Bound ISBN 1594899-56-8

Volume 4 features the Lydian scale in all twelve keys; two octaves up and down with complete piano fingerings. Chords are presented with left hand voicings that work with the scale (along with fingerings) Also included are exercises to develop the concept of melodic phrasing in improvisation, examples of the use of the Lydian scale in the jazz repertoire, and detailed instructions on how to practice the material. Added feature: author can be contacted online if questions arise.

Jazz Piano Vocabulary by Roberta Piket, Volume 5: The Mixolydian Mode
Spiral Bound ISBN 1594899-57-6   Perfect Bound ISBN 1594899-58-4

This book focuses on the Mixolydian scale and applies it to improvising on dominant seventh and dominant seventh sus chords. The scale is presented in all twelve keys with fingerings. The book also contains an introduction to approach notes, an explanation and étude on twelve bar blues form, left hand voicings, exercises, melodic examples, instruction and practice tips.

Guitar Method Series

This series of books distills several of our previous publications into a method currently in use at New York University for the Summer Guitar Intensive Program. Content is geared towards any musician that is looking to expand their understanding of typical musical concepts but also covers many musically uncharted territories. Material concentrates on essential information the student must master in order to become a professional guitarist in the heavily competitive New York City music scene. This series of books starts with the most basic beginning guitar information and takes the reader to the most advanced musical concepts.

New York Guitar Method Primer Book 1
Spiral Bound ISBN 159489-911-8   Perfect Bound ISBN 159489-912-6

This book provides students with an excellent foundation in theory, ear training, chord and scale comprehension on the guitar. It is a prerequisite for entering New York University's Summer Guitar Intensive Program and provides students studying independently with the tools they will need to successfully move on to Primer Book 2.

New York Guitar Method Primer Book 2
Spiral Bound ISBN 159489-915-0   Perfect Bound ISBN 159489-916-9

This book provides students with an excellent foundation in theory, ear training, chord and scale comprehension on the guitar. It is a prerequisite for entering New York University's Summer Guitar Intensive Program and provides students studying independently with the tools they will need to successfully move on to New York Guitar Method Book 1.   "New York Guitar Method Primer Ensemble Book Two" is the companion book for "New York Guitar Method Primer Book Two." This book contains music examples of the information covered in this book so that a student can apply the information through memorization and sight reading.

New York Guitar Method Primer Ensemble Book 2
Spiral Bound ISBN 159489-913-4   Perfect Bound ISBN 159489-914-2

This book is a prerequisite for entering New York University's Summer Guitar Intensive Program and provides students studying independently with the tools they will need to successfully move on to Volume 1. Our Ensemble Method presents a breakthrough approach for teaching guitarist how to sightread. Each chapter has eighth note, sixteenth note, single string, lines, and chord exercises. The book also includes modal jazz vamps and solos and is an excellent resource for lab/ensemble studies as it contains 3 and 4-part reading examples.

New York Guitar Method Volume 1
Spiral Bound ISBN 159489-987-8   Perfect Bound ISBN 159489-900-2

This book contains 22 scales and their theory which are covered in great detail. Multiple types of chord voicings along with an in-Depth coverage of articulations. The application of scales through modal sequences is also explained. The following musical concepts are covered: Finding the Right Scale for Any Chord, Finding the Natural Scale Sound, Thinking the Way You Hear, Two to Eleven Note Scale Possibilities along with a list of 2,048 Scale Possibilities which contain the root. Slash Chords, Regular Chords and Slash Chords, Slash Chord Possibilities, Reharmonization Theory, Adding Tensions.
"New York Guitar Method Ensemble Book One" is the companion book for "New York Guitar Method Volume One." This book contains music examples of the information covered in this book so that a student can apply the information through memorization and sight reading.

New York Guitar Method Ensemble Book 1
Spiral Bound ISBN 159489-905-3   Perfect Bound ISBN 159489-906-1

Volume One focuses on reading jazz solos that demonstrate the many uses of scales as discussed in the accompanying New York Guitar Method Volume 1. The book also includes jazz and classical reading études and is an excellent resource for lab/ensemble studies as it contains 3 and 4-part reading examples.

New York Guitar Method Volume 2
Spiral Bound ISBN 159489-901-0   Perfect Bound ISBN 159489-902-9

This is the second book in our series currently in use at New York University for the Summer Guitar Intensive Program. A continuation of Volume 1, Volume 2 focuses on approach notes and discusses how to apply approaches to jazz lines in order to create the signature sounding lines of bebop through the contemporary sounding lines of the modern masters. "New York Guitar Method Ensemble Book Two" is the companion book for "New York Guitar Method Volume Two." This book contains music examples of the information covered in this book so that a student can apply the information through memorization and sight reading.

New York Guitar Method Ensemble Book 2
Spiral Bound ISBN 159489-907-X   Perfect Bound ISBN 159489-908-8

Volume Two focuses on reading jazz solos that demonstrate the many uses of approach notes as discussed in the accompanying New York Guitar Method Volume 2. The book also includes jazz and classical reading études and is an excellent resource for lab/ensemble studies as it contains 3 and 4-part reading examples.

Set Theory Method

This series of books explores the relationships of post tonal theory to contemporary improvisation. It is meant to bridge the gap between jazz theory and contemporary set theory.

Sonic Resource Guide
Spiral Bound ISBN 159489-933-9   Perfect Bound ISBN 159489-934-7

"Set Theory for Improvisation" examines the use and organization of pitch class sets for improvisation and composition. Two through twelve note pitch class sets are explored and their application to the harmony and melody shown through multiple examples. The companion series "Set Theory for Improvisation Ensemble" is recommended as both a overall musical development tool and as a sight reading gold mine. For all instruments.

Set Theory for Improvisation Ensemble Method

The ensemble method gives examples of applying post tonal theory to contemporary improvisation in the form of études. Each étude explores the melodic possibilities using various combinations of note groupings, rhythms, metric level, melodic range and density. There are 12 études in each book, one in each key which can be played over a variety of chords. These études range from highly diatonic to non-diatonic examples depending on the organization of the material. For all instruments.

Set Theory for Improvisation Ensemble Method: Hexatonic 027 027
Spiral Bound ISBN 159489-920-7   Perfect Bound ISBN 159489-921-5

Set Theory for Improvisation Ensemble Method: Hexatonic 027 016
Spiral Bound ISBN 159489-922-3   Perfect Bound ISBN 159489-923-1

Set Theory for Improvisation Ensemble Method: Hexatonic 027 026
Spiral Bound ISBN 159489-924-X   Perfect Bound ISBN 159489-925-8

E-Books

The Bruce Arnold series of instructional E-books is for the student who wishes to target specific areas of study that are of particular interest. Many of these books are excerpted from other larger texts. The excerpted source is listed for each book. These books are available on-line at www.muse-eek.com as well as at many e-tailers throughout the internet. These books can also be purchased in the traditional book binding format. (See the ISBN number for proper format)

Chord Velocity: Volume One, Learning to switch between chords quickly
E-book ISBN 1-890944-88-2   Traditional Book Binding ISBN 1-890944-97-1

The first hurdle a beginning guitarist encounters is difficulty in switching between chords quickly enough to make a chord progression sound like music. This book provides exercises that help a student gradually increase the speed with which they change chords. Special free audio files are also available on the muse-eek.com website to make practice more productive and fun. Within a few weeks, remarkable improvement can be achieved using this method. This book is excerpted from "1st Steps for a Beginning Guitarist Volume One."

Guitar Technique: Volume One, Learning the basics to fast, clean, accurate and fluid performance skills.
E-book ISBN 1-890944-91-2   Traditional Book Binding ISBN 1-890944-99-8

This book is for both the beginning guitarist or the more experienced guitarist who wishes to improve their technique. All aspects of the physical act of playing the guitar are covered, from how to hold a guitar to the specific way each hand is involved in the playing process. Pictures and videos are provided to help clarify each technique. These pictures and videos are either contained in the book or can be downloaded at www.muse-eek.com This book is excerpted from "1st Steps for a Beginning Guitarist Volume One."

Accompaniment: Volume One, Learning to Play Bass and Chords Simultaneously
E-book ISBN 1-890944-87-4   Traditional Book Binding ISBN 1-890944-96-3

The techniques found within this book are an excellent resource for creating and understanding how to play bass and chords simultaneously in a jazz or blues style. Special attention is paid to understanding how this technique is created, thereby enabling the student to recreate this style with other pieces of music. This book is excerpted from the book "Guitar Clinic."

Beginning Rhythm Studies: Volume One, Learning the basics of reading rhythm and playing in time.
E-book ISBN 1-890944-89-0   Traditional Book Binding 1-890944-98-X

This book covers the basics for anyone wishing to understand or improve their rhythmic abilities. Simple language is used to show the student how to read and play rhythm. Exercises are presented which can accelerate the learning process. Audio examples in the form of midifiles are available on the muse-eek.com website to facilitate learning the correct rhythm in time. This book is excerpted from the book "Rhythm Primer."

www.ingramcontent.com/pod-product-compliance
Lightning Source LLC
Chambersburg PA
CBHW080344170426
43194CB00014B/2676